POPULAR
SONGS
HAL LEONARD
STUDENT PIANO LIBRARY

EARLY INTERMEDIATE / INTERMEDIATE

Video Game Hits
for Easy Piano

Arranged by Mona Rejino

ISBN 978-1-5400-6246-8

Visit Hal Leonard Online at
www.halleonard.com

Contact us:
Hal Leonard
7777 West Bluemound Road
Milwaukee, WI 53213
Email: info@halleonard.com

In Europe, contact:
Hal Leonard Europe Limited
42 Wigmore Street
Marylebone, London, W1U 2RN
Email: info@halleonardeurope.com

In Australia, contact:
Hal Leonard Australia Pty. Ltd.
4 Lentara Court
Cheltenham, Victoria, 3192 Australia
Email: info@halleonard.com.au

From the Arranger

In taking on the project of arranging video game music, I found that there is both amazing variety and depth in these beloved pieces. "Angry Birds" has a quirky, catchy, rhythmic theme that keeps running through your head. "Bratja" from *Full Metal Alchemist* has a haunting, expressive melody. "Dearly Beloved" from *Kingdom Hearts* has a theme that is continuous and never-ending, like a circle. "Dragonborn" has a heroic nature propelled by a driving rhythm and forward motion. "Eyes on Me" from *Final Fantasy VIII* is a tender, warm, lovely piece of music. "Main Theme" from *Final Fantasy I* is quietly regal, yet also majestic. "Sadness and Sorrow" from *Naruto* has a lyrical melody that leaves you wanting to know more.

It is hard to imagine video games without music, which is such an integral part of the whole experience. The music contained in this book dates from 1987 to 2011, spanning a whole generation. May you find happy memories and musical fulfillment in these special pieces.

Mona Rejino

An accomplished pianist, composer, arranger, and teacher, **Mona Rejino** maintains an independent piano studio in Carrollton, Texas. She also teaches privately at the Hockaday School and is a frequent adjudicator in the Dallas area. A member of *Who's Who of American Women*, Mona received her music degrees from West Texas State University and the University of North Texas. She and her husband, Richard, often present programs on a variety of topics for music teacher associations throughout Texas as well as nationally.

CONTENTS

Angry Birds Theme

By Ari Pulkkinen
Arranged by Mona Rejino

Oom-pah style (♩ = 100)

6

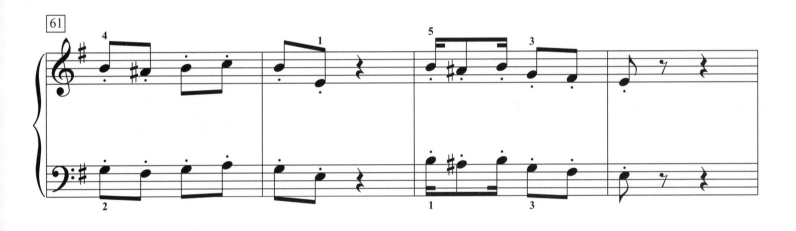

Bratja

(Brothers)
from FULL METAL ALCHEMIST

Words and Music by Michiru Oshima,
Seiji Mizushima and Tatiana Naumova
Arranged by Mona Rejino

Dearly Beloved

from KINGDOM HEARTS

Music by Yoko Shimomura
Arranged by Mona Rejino

Moderately slow (♩ = 60)

R.H. 8va throughout

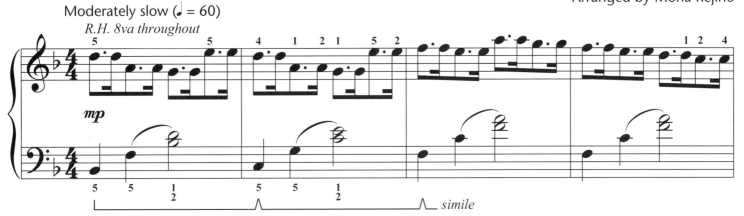

Dragonborn
(Skyrim Theme)

By Jeremy Soule
Arranged by Mona Rejino

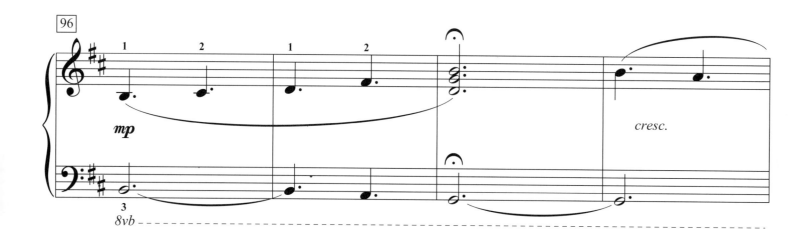

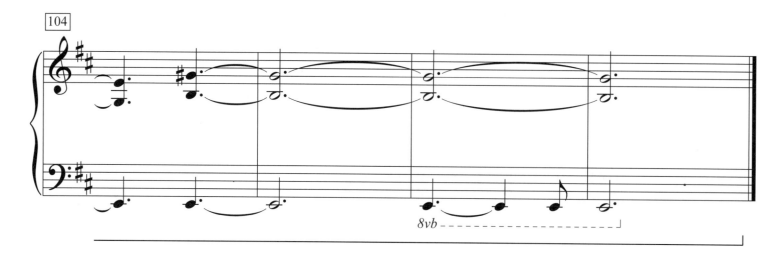

Eyes on Me
from FINAL FANTASY VIII

Music by Nobuo Uematsu
Lyrics by Kako Someya
Arranged by Mona Rejino

Moderately slow, with freedom (♩ = 80)

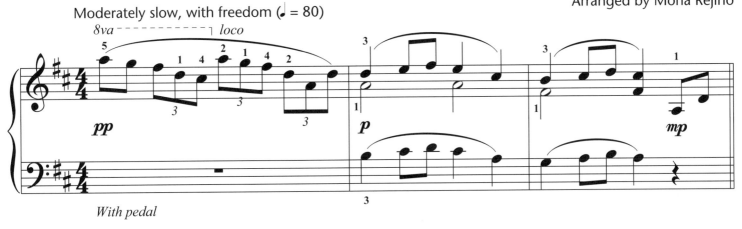

With pedal

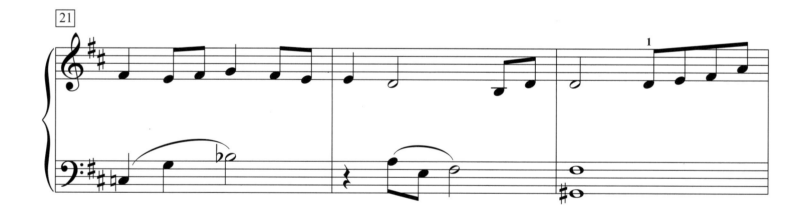

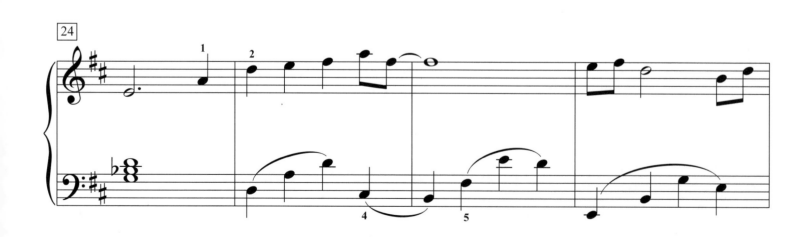

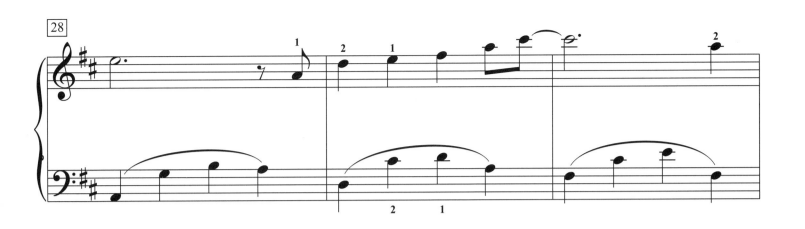

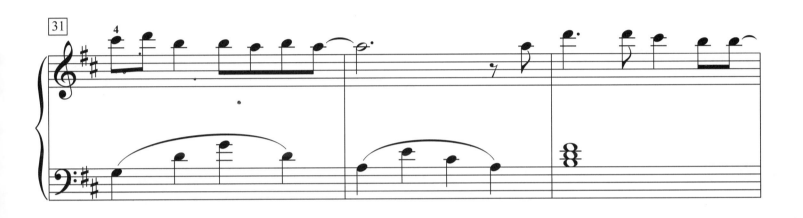

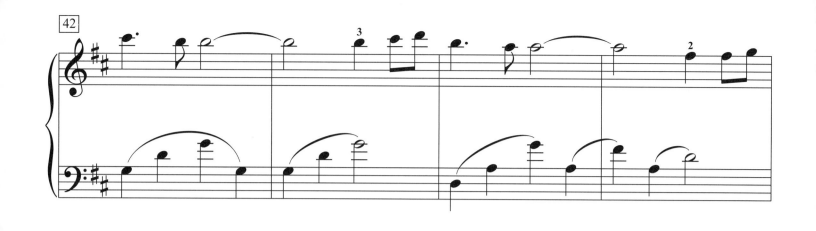

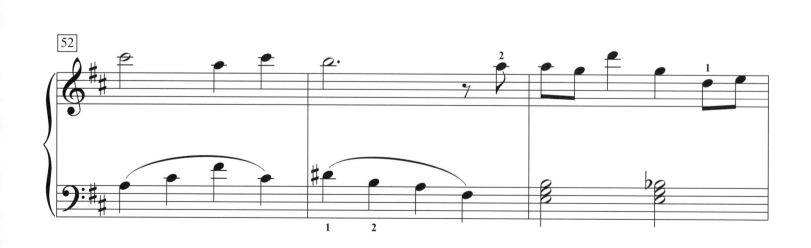

24

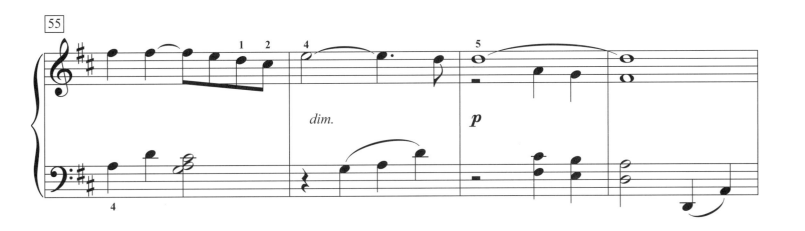

Main Theme

from FINAL FANTASY I

By Nobuo Uematsu
Arranged by Mona Rejino

Majestically, slightly slower

Sadness and Sorrow

from the television series NARUTO

By Purojekuto Musashi
Arranged by Mona Rejino

Lento (♩ = 63)

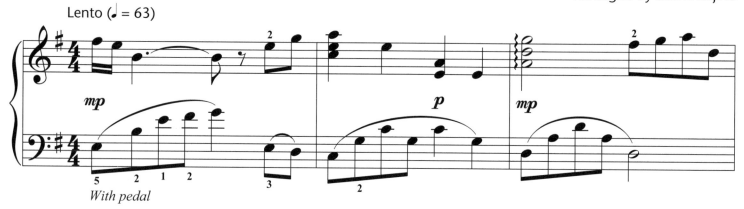

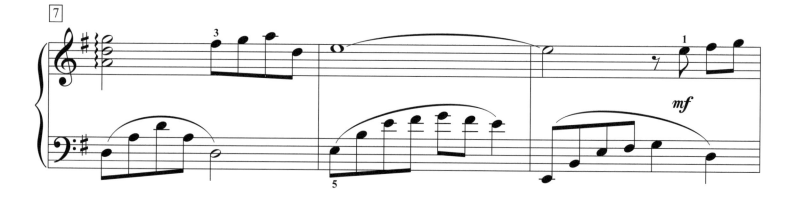

POPULAR SONGS
HAL LEONARD STUDENT PIANO LIBRARY

The **Hal Leonard Student Piano Library** has great songs, and you will find all your favorites here: Disney classics, Broadway and movie favorites, and today's top hits. These graded collections are skillfully and imaginatively arranged for students and pianists at every level, from elementary solos with teacher accompaniments to sophisticated piano solos for the advancing pianist.

Adele
arr. Mona Rejino
Correlates with HLSPL Level 5
00159590...............................$12.99

The Beatles
arr. Eugénie Rocherolle
Correlates with HLSPL Level 5
00296649............................. $12.99

Irving Berlin Piano Duos
arr. Don Heitler and Jim Lyke
Correlates with HLSPL Level 5
00296838...............................$14.99

Broadway Favorites
arr. Phillip Keveren
Correlates with HLSPL Level 4
00279192...............................$12.99

Chart Hits
arr. Mona Rejino
Correlates with HLSPL Level 5
00296710...............................$8.99

Christmas at the Piano
arr. Lynda Lybeck-Robinson
Correlates with HLSPL Level 4
00298194...............................$12.99

Christmas Cheer
arr. Phillip Keveren
Correlates with HLSPL Level 4
00296616...............................$8.99

Classic Christmas Favorites
arr. Jennifer & Mike Watts
Correlates with HLSPL Level 5
00129582...............................$9.99

Christmas Time Is Here
arr. Eugénie Rocherolle
Correlates with HLSPL Level 5
00296614...............................$8.99

Classic Joplin Rags
arr. Fred Kern
Correlates with HLSPL Level 5
00296743...............................$9.99

Classical Pop – Lady Gaga Fugue & Other Pop Hits
arr. Giovanni Dettori
Correlates with HLSPL Level 5
00296921...............................$12.99

Contemporary Movie Hits
arr. by Carol Klose, Jennifer Linn and Wendy Stevens
Correlates with HLSPL Level 5
00296780...............................$8.99

Contemporary Pop Hits
arr. Wendy Stevens
Correlates with HLSPL Level 3
00296836...............................$8.99

Cool Pop
arr. Mona Rejino
Correlates with HLSPL Level 5
00360103...............................$12.99

Country Favorites
arr. Mona Rejino
Correlates with HLSPL Level 5
00296861...............................$9.99

Disney Favorites
arr. Phillip Keveren
Correlates with HLSPL Levels 3/4
00296647...............................$10.99

Disney Film Favorites
arr. Mona Rejino
Correlates with HLSPL Level 5
00296809 ....$10.99

Disney Piano Duets
arr. Jennifer & Mike Watts
Correlates with HLSPL Level 5
00113759...............................$13.99

Double Agent! Piano Duets
arr. Jeremy Siskind
Correlates with HLSPL Level 5
00121595...............................$12.99

Easy Christmas Duets
arr. Mona Rejino & Phillip Keveren
Correlates with HLSPL Levels 3/4
00237139...............................$9.99

Easy Disney Duets
arr. Jennifer and Mike Watts
Correlates with HLSPL Level 4
00243727...............................$12.99

Four Hands on Broadway
arr. Fred Kern
Correlates with HLSPL Level 5
00146177...............................$12.99

Frozen Piano Duets
arr. Mona Rejino
Correlates with HLSPL Levels 3/4
00144294...............................$12.99

Hip-Hop for Piano Solo
arr. Logan Evan Thomas
Correlates with HLSPL Level 5
00360950...............................$12.99

Jazz Hits for Piano Duet
arr. Jeremy Siskind
Correlates with HLSPL Level 5
00143248...............................$12.99

Elton John
arr. Carol Klose
Correlates with HLSPL Level 5
00296721...............................$10.99

Joplin Ragtime Duets
arr. Fred Kern
Correlates with HLSPL Level 5
00296771...............................$8.99

Movie Blockbusters
arr. Mona Rejino
Correlates with HLSPL Level 5
00232850...............................$10.99

The Nutcracker Suite
arr. Lynda Lybeck-Robinson
Correlates with HLSPL Levels 3/4
00147906...............................$8.99

Pop Hits for Piano Duet
arr. Jeremy Siskind
Correlates with HLSPL Level 5
00224734...............................$12.99

Sing to the King
arr. Phillip Keveren
Correlates with HLSPL Level 5
00296808...............................$8.99

Smash Hits
arr. Mona Rejino
Correlates with HLSPL Level 5
00284841...............................$10.99

Spooky Halloween Tunes
arr. Fred Kern
Correlates with HLSPL Levels 3/4
00121550...............................$9.99

Today's Hits
arr. Mona Rejino
Correlates with HLSPL Level 5
00296646...............................$9.99

Top Hits
arr. Jennifer and Mike Watts
Correlates with HLSPL Level 5
00296894...............................$10.99

Top Piano Ballads
arr. Jennifer Watts
Correlates with HLSPL Level 5
00197926...............................$10.99

Video Game Hits
arr. Mona Rejino
Correlates with HLSPL Level 4
00300310...............................$12.99

You Raise Me Up
arr. Deborah Brady
Correlates with HLSPL Level 2/3
00296576...............................$7.95